P9-AFZ-564

SandCastle™
Animal Groups

A Streak
of Tigers

ANIMAL GROUPS
IN THE JUNGLE

Alex Kuskowski

CONSULTING EDITOR, DIANE CRAIG, M.A./READING SPECIALIST

A Division of ABDO
ABDO
Publishing Company

visit us at www.abdopublishing.com

Published by ABDO Publishing Company, a division of ABDO, P.O. Box 398166, Minneapolis, Minnesota 55439. Copyright © 2013 by Abdo Consulting Group, Inc. International copyrights reserved in all countries. No part of this book may be reproduced in any form without written permission from the publisher. SandCastle™ is a trademark and logo of ABDO Publishing Company.

Printed in the United States of America, North Mankato, Minnesota
062012
092012

 PRINTED ON RECYCLED PAPER

Editor: Liz Salzmann
Content Developer: Nancy Tuminelly
Cover and Interior Design and Production: Anders Hanson, Mighty Media, Inc.
Photo Credits: Shutterstock

Library of Congress Cataloging-in-Publication Data
Kuskowski, Alex.
  A streak of tigers : animal groups in the jungle / Alex Kuskowski.
     p. cm. -- (Animal groups)
  ISBN 978-1-61783-542-1
  1. Jungle animals--Behavior--Juvenile literature. 2. Social behavior in animals--Juvenile literature. I. Title.
  QL112.K873 2013
  599.1734--dc23
                    2012009607

SANDCASTLE™ LEVEL: FLUENT

SandCastle™ books are created by a team of professional educators, reading specialists, and content developers around five essential components—phonemic awareness, phonics, vocabulary, text comprehension, and fluency—to assist young readers as they develop reading skills and strategies and increase their general knowledge. All books are written, reviewed, and leveled for guided reading, early reading intervention, and Accelerated Reader® programs for use in shared, guided, and independent reading and writing activities to support a balanced approach to literacy instruction. The SandCastle™ series has four levels that correspond to early literacy development. The levels are provided to help teachers and parents select appropriate books for young readers.

Emerging Readers	Beginning Readers	Transitional Readers	Fluent Readers
(no flags)	*(1 flag)*	*(2 flags)*	*(3 flags)*

Contents

Animals in the Jungle

A jungle is an area with a lot of plants and trees. Most jungles are **tropical**. Many wild animals live in the jungle. Thick plants make animals feel safe. The plants also give many animals food to eat.

Why Live in a Group?

Animals often live in groups. Animals in a group can **protect** each other. They can share space, food, and water. They also work together to help raise babies. Many animal groups have fun names!

A Leap of Leopards

A mother leopard and her cubs are called a leap. Cubs live with their mother until they are two years old. She teaches them how to hunt **prey** in the jungle.

Leopard Names

MALE	FEMALE	BABY	GROUP
leopard	leopardess	cub	leap, prowl

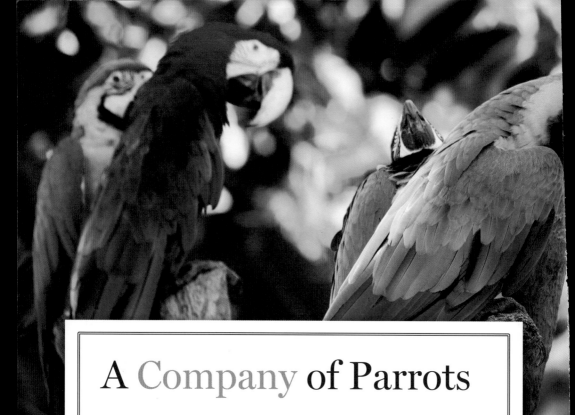

A Company of Parrots

Macaws are a type of parrot. They live together in a company. During the day they **forage** for fruits and nuts.

Parrot Names

MALE	FEMALE	BABY	GROUP
cock	*hen*	*chick*	*company, flock*

A Congress of Lemurs

A group of lemurs is called a congress. They sit in a line and **groom** each other. It helps them to stay clean.

Lemur Names

MALE
dictator

FEMALE
princess

BABY
infant

GROUP
congress, troop

14

A Shrewdness of Apes

Gibbons are apes that live in the jungle. A shrewdness of gibbons will sing together very loudly. Their song can be heard a mile away. It warns other gibbons to stay away.

Ape Names

MALE
male

FEMALE
female

BABY
baby, infant

GROUP
shrewdness, family

A Bask of Crocodiles

A group of crocodiles is called a bask. Crocodiles are found in the rivers of the Amazon jungle. Many crocodiles **compete** for fish and space.

Crocodile Names

MALE	FEMALE	BABY	GROUP
bull	*cow*	*hatchling*	*bask, float*

A Tribe of Monkeys

Macaque monkeys live in a tribe. During the winter, they warm up in **hot springs**.

Monkey Names

MALE
male

FEMALE
female

BABY
infant

GROUP
tribe, troop

A Streak of Tigers

A mother tiger and her cubs are a streak of tigers. Tigers usually have between two and six cubs.

Tiger Names

MALE
tiger

FEMALE
tigress

BABY
cub

GROUP
streak, ambush

More
JUNGLE GROUPS

A flutter of
butterflies

A wisdom
of wombats

A lounge
of lizards

A colony
of bats

A den of
snakes

A crash
of rhinos

Quiz

1. All jungles are **tropical**.
True or false?

2. Leopard cubs live with their mother until they are 10 years old.
True or false?

3. The gibbons' song can be heard a mile away. *True or false?*

4. Macaque monkeys warm up in **hot springs**. *True or false?*

5. Tigers usually have eight cubs.
True or false?

Glossary

compete – to try hard to outdo others in achieving a goal.

forage – to search for food.

groom – to clean the fur of an animal.

hot spring – a place where hot water comes up out of the ground.

prey – an animal that is hunted or caught for food.

protect – to guard someone or something from harm or danger.

tropical – located in one of the hottest areas on earth.